The Prayer MAP® for DIFFICULT TIMES

BARBOUR
PUBLISHING

Published by Barbour Publishing, Inc., 1810 Barbour Drive, Uhrichsville, Ohio 44683, www.barbourbooks.com

Our mission is to inspire the world with the life-changing message of the Bible.

Member of the
Evangelical Christian
Publishers Association

Printed in China.

WHAT DOES A LIFE OF JOY AND SERENITY— DESPITE DIFFICULT TIMES— LOOK LIKE? . . .

Get ready to experience the peace and contentment that only the heavenly Creator can provide with this creative journal. . .where every colorful page will guide you to create your very own comforting prayer map—as you write out specific thoughts, ideas, and lists, which you can follow (from start to finish!)—as you talk to God. (Be sure to record the date on each one of your prayer maps so you can look back over time and see how God has continued to work in your life!)

The Prayer Map for Difficult Times will not only encourage you to spend time talking with God about life's tough situations. . .it will also help you build a healthy spiritual habit of continual prayer for life!

Date:

DEAR HEAVENLY FATHER,

....
....
....
....

*Today my heart is
troubled because. . .*

....
....
....
....
....
....
....
....
....
....
....
....
....
....

*(but with You by my side,
I am comforted!)*

I'M FEELING. . .

....
....
....
....
....
....
....
....
....
....
....
....
....
....
....

I NEED YOUR HELP TO...

....
....
....
....
....
....
....
....
....
....
....
....
....
....
....

Even when life is difficult, You provide many blessings, including...

....
....
....
....
....
....
....

Thank You, Father, for hearing my prayers.

AMEN.

As for God, his way is perfect: the LORD's word is flawless; he shields all who take refuge in him.

PSALM 18:30 NIV

Date:

DEAR HEAVENLY FATHER,

Today my heart is troubled because. . .

I'M FEELING. . .

(but with You by my side, I am comforted!)

I NEED YOUR HELP TO...

....

....

....

....

....

....

....

....

....

....

....

....

....

Even when life is difficult, You provide many blessings, including...

....

....

....

....

....

....

....

Thank You, Father, for hearing my prayers.
AMEN.

He tends his flock like a shepherd: he gathers the lambs in his arms and carries them close to his heart.
ISAIAH 40:11 NIV

 Date:

DEAR HEAVENLY FATHER,

Today my heart is
troubled because. . .

I'M FEELING. . .

(but with You by my side,
I am comforted!)

I NEED YOUR HELP TO...

....

....

....

....

....

....

....

....

....

....

....

....

....

Even when life is difficult, You provide many blessings, including...

....

....

....

....

....

....

....

Thank You, Father, for hearing my prayers.
AMEN.

"The Lord your God is with you, the Mighty Warrior who saves."
ZEPHANIAH 3:17 NIV

 Date:

DEAR HEAVENLY FATHER,

Today my heart is troubled because. . .

(but with You by my side, I am comforted!)

I'M FEELING. . .

I NEED YOUR HELP TO...

....
....
....
....
....
....
....
....
....
....
....
....
....
....

Even when life is difficult, You provide many blessings, including...

....
....
....
....
....
....
....
....
....

Thank You, Father, for hearing my prayers.
AMEN.

"The LORD himself goes before you and will be with you; he will never leave you nor forsake you. Do not be afraid; do not be discouraged."

DEUTERONOMY 31:8 NIV

 Date:

DEAR HEAVENLY FATHER,

Today my heart is troubled because. . .

(but with You by my side, I am comforted!)

I'M FEELING. . .

I NEED YOUR HELP TO. . .

....

....

....

....

....

....

....

....

....

....

....

....

Even when life is difficult, You provide many blessings, including. . .

....

....

....

....

....

....

....

....

Thank You, Father, for hearing my prayers.
AMEN.

Now faith is confidence in what we hope for and assurance about what we do not see.
HEBREWS 11:1 NIV

Date:

DEAR HEAVENLY FATHER,

Today my heart is troubled because. . .

(but with You by my side, I am comforted!)

I'M FEELING. . .

I NEED YOUR HELP TO...

....
....
....
....
....
....
....
....
....
....
....
....
....
....

Even when life is difficult, You provide many blessings, including...

....
....
....
....
....
....
....

Thank You, Father, for hearing my prayers.
AMEN.

But let all who take refuge in you rejoice; let them sing joyful praises forever. Spread your protection over them, that all who love your name may be filled with joy.
PSALM 5:11 NLT

Date:

DEAR HEAVENLY FATHER,

....

....

....

....

Today my heart is troubled because. . .

....

....

....

....

....

....

....

....

....

....

....

(but with You by my side, I am comforted!)

I'M FEELING. . .

....

....

....

....

....

....

....

....

....

....

....

....

....

....

I NEED YOUR HELP TO...

....
....
....
....
....
....
....
....
....
....
....
....
....
....

Even when life is difficult, You provide many blessings, including...

....
....
....
....
....
....
....

Thank You, Father, for hearing my prayers.
AMEN.

Finally, brothers and sisters, whatever is true, whatever is noble, whatever is right, whatever is pure, whatever is lovely, whatever is admirable—if anything is excellent or praiseworthy—think about such things.

PHILIPPIANS 4:8 NIV

 Date:

DEAR HEAVENLY FATHER,

Today my heart is troubled because. . .

(but with You by my side, I am comforted!)

I'M FEELING. . .

I NEED YOUR HELP TO...

....
....
....
....
....
....
....
....
....
....
....
....
....
....
....
....
....

Even when life is difficult, You provide many blessings, including...

....
....
....
....
....
....
....
....
....
....
....

Thank You, Father, for hearing my prayers.
AMEN.

I waited patiently for the LORD; he turned to me and heard my cry. He lifted me out of the slimy pit, out of the mud and mire; he set my feet on a rock and gave me a firm place to stand. He put a new song in my mouth, a hymn of praise to our God.

PSALM 40:1–3 NIV

 Date:

DEAR HEAVENLY FATHER,

....

....

....

....

Today my heart is troubled because. . .

....

....

....

....

....

....

....

....

....

....

....

....

(but with You by my side, I am comforted!)

I'M FEELING. . .

....

....

....

....

....

....

....

....

....

....

....

....

....

I NEED YOUR HELP TO...

....
....
....
....
....
....
....
....
....
....
....
....
....
....

Even when life is difficult, You provide many blessings, including...

....
....
....
....
....
....
....
....

Thank You, Father, for hearing my prayers.
AMEN.

Many are the afflictions of the righteous, but the LORD delivers him out of them all.
PSALM 34:19 ESV

 Date:

DEAR HEAVENLY FATHER,

Today my heart is troubled because. . .

(but with You by my side, I am comforted!)

I'M FEELING. . .

I NEED YOUR HELP TO...

....

....

....

....

....

....

....

....

....

....

....

....

....

....

Even when life is difficult, You provide many blessings, including...

....

....

....

....

....

....

....

....

Thank You, Father, for hearing my prayers.

AMEN.

"You, LORD, are my lamp;
the LORD turns my darkness into light."
2 SAMUEL 22:29 NIV

Date:

DEAR HEAVENLY FATHER,

Today my heart is troubled because. . .

I'M FEELING. . .

(but with You by my side, I am comforted!)

I NEED YOUR HELP TO. . .

....
....
....
....
....
....
....
....
....
....
....
....
....
....
....
....

Even when life is difficult, You provide many blessings, including. . .

....
....
....
....
....
....
....
....
....
....

Thank You, Father, for hearing my prayers.
AMEN.

Be anxious for nothing, but in everything by prayer and supplication with thanksgiving let your requests be made known to God. And the peace of God, which surpasses all comprehension, will guard your hearts and your minds in Christ Jesus.

PHILIPPIANS 4:6–7 NASB

Date:

DEAR HEAVENLY FATHER,

....

....

....

....

*Today my heart is
troubled because. . .*

....

....

....

....

....

....

....

....

....

....

....

....

*(but with You by my side,
I am comforted!)*

I'M FEELING. . .

....

....

....

....

....

....

....

....

....

....

....

....

....

....

I NEED YOUR HELP TO...

....
....
....
....
....
....
....
....
....
....
....
....
....

Even when life is difficult, You provide many blessings, including...

....
....
....
....
....
....
....
....

Thank You, Father, for hearing my prayers.
AMEN.

"Let not your heart be troubled."
JOHN 14:1 NKJV

Date:

DEAR HEAVENLY FATHER,

....

....

....

....

*Today my heart is
troubled because. . .*

....

....

....

....

....

....

....

....

....

....

....

....

*(but with You by my side,
I am comforted!)*

I'M FEELING. . .

....

....

....

....

....

....

....

....

....

....

....

....

....

....

I NEED YOUR HELP TO...

....
....
....
....
....
....
....
....
....
....
....
....
....
....
....

Even when life is difficult, You provide many blessings, including...

....
....
....
....
....
....
....

Thank You, Father, for hearing my prayers.
AMEN.

For he will deliver the needy when he cries for help, the afflicted also, and him who has no helper.
PSALM 72:12 NASB

 Date:

DEAR HEAVENLY FATHER,

....

....

....

....

*Today my heart is
troubled because. . .*

....

....

....

....

....

....

....

....

....

....

....

*(but with You by my side,
I am comforted!)*

I'M FEELING. . .

....

....

....

....

....

....

....

....

....

....

....

....

....

I NEED YOUR HELP TO...

....
....
....
....
....
....
....
....
....
....
....
....
....
....
....
....
....
....
....

Even when life is difficult, You provide many blessings, including...

....
....
....
....
....
....
....
....
....
....

Thank You, Father, for hearing my prayers.
AMEN.

Your lovingkindness, O LORD, will hold me up. When my anxious thoughts multiply within me, Your consolations delight my soul.

PSALM 94:18–19 NASB

Date:

DEAR HEAVENLY FATHER,

Today my heart is troubled because. . .

I'M FEELING. . .

(but with You by my side, I am comforted!)

I NEED YOUR HELP TO...

....
....
....
....
....
....
....
....
....
....
....
....
....
....
....

Even when life is difficult, You provide many blessings, including...

....
....
....
....
....
....
....

*Thank You, Father,
for hearing my prayers.*
AMEN.

*I sought the LORD, and He answered me,
and delivered me from all my fears.*
PSALM 34:4 NASB

Date:

DEAR HEAVENLY FATHER,

Today my heart is troubled because. . .

(but with You by my side, I am comforted!)

I'M FEELING. . .

I NEED YOUR HELP TO...

....
....
....
....
....
....
....
....
....
....
....
....
....
....
....
....
....
....

Even when life is difficult, You provide many blessings, including...

....
....
....
....
....
....
....
....
....

Thank You, Father, for hearing my prayers.
AMEN.

Let us then with confidence draw near to the throne of grace, that we may receive mercy and find grace to help in time of need.
HEBREWS 4:16 ESV

 Date:

DEAR HEAVENLY FATHER,

Today my heart is troubled because. . .

(but with You by my side, I am comforted!)

I'M FEELING. . .

I NEED YOUR HELP TO...

....
....
....
....
....
....
....
....
....
....
....
....
....
....

Even when life is difficult, You provide many blessings, including...

....
....
....
....
....
....
....
....

Thank You, Father, for hearing my prayers.
AMEN.

Commit your way to the LORD; trust in him, and he will act.
PSALM 37:5 NRSV

Date:

DEAR HEAVENLY FATHER,

Today my heart is troubled because. . .

(but with You by my side, I am comforted!)

I'M FEELING. . .

I NEED YOUR HELP TO...

....

....

....

....

....

....

....

....

....

....

....

....

....

Even when life is difficult, You provide many blessings, including...

....

....

....

....

....

....

....

....

Thank You, Father, for hearing my prayers.
AMEN.

The LORD's unfailing love surrounds the one who trusts in him.
PSALM 32:10 NIV

 Date:

DEAR HEAVENLY FATHER,

Today my heart is troubled because. . .

(but with You by my side, I am comforted!)

I'M FEELING. . .

I NEED YOUR HELP TO...

....

....

....

....

....

....

....

....

....

....

....

....

....

....

....

Even when life is difficult, You provide many blessings, including...

....

....

....

....

....

....

....

....

Thank You, Father, for hearing my prayers.

AMEN.

I can do all this through him who gives me strength.
PHILIPPIANS 4:13 NIV

Date:

DEAR HEAVENLY FATHER,

....

....

....

....

Today my heart is troubled because. . .

....

....

....

....

....

....

....

....

....

....

(but with You by my side, I am comforted!)

I'M FEELING. . .

....

....

....

....

....

....

....

....

....

....

....

....

....

....

I NEED YOUR HELP TO. . .

....
....
....
....
....
....
....
....
....
....
....
....
....
....
....
....
....
....
....

Even when life is difficult, You provide many blessings, including. . .

....
....
....
....
....
....
....
....
....
....
....

Thank You, Father, for hearing my prayers.
AMEN.

Humble yourselves, therefore, under God's mighty hand, that he may lift you up in due time. Cast all your anxiety on him because he cares for you.
1 PETER 5:6–7 NIV

 Date:

DEAR HEAVENLY FATHER,

Today my heart is troubled because. . .

(but with You by my side, I am comforted!)

I'M FEELING. . .

I NEED YOUR HELP TO...

....

....

....

....

....

....

....

....

....

....

....

....

....

Even when life is difficult, You provide many blessings, including...

....

....

....

....

....

....

Thank You, Father, for hearing my prayers.
AMEN.

For everyone who has been born of God overcomes the world. And this is the victory that has overcome the world—our faith.
1 JOHN 5:4 ESV

Date:

DEAR HEAVENLY FATHER,

Today my heart is troubled because. . .

(but with You by my side, I am comforted!)

I'M FEELING. . .

I NEED YOUR HELP TO...

....
....
....
....
....
....
....
....
....
....
....
....
....

Even when life is difficult, You provide many blessings, including...

....
....
....
....
....
....
....

Thank You, Father, for hearing my prayers.
AMEN.

The prayer of a righteous person has great power as it is working.
JAMES 5:16 ESV

 Date:

DEAR HEAVENLY FATHER,

Today my heart is troubled because. . .

(but with You by my side, I am comforted!)

I'M FEELING. . .

I NEED YOUR HELP TO...

....

....

....

....

....

....

....

....

....

....

....

....

....

Even when life is difficult, You provide many blessings, including...

....

....

....

....

....

Thank You, Father, for hearing my prayers.
AMEN.

"Peace I leave with you; my peace I give to you. I do not give to you as the world gives. Do not let your hearts be troubled, and do not let them be afraid."
JOHN 14:27 NRSV

 Date:

DEAR HEAVENLY FATHER,

....
....
....
....

Today my heart is troubled because. . .

....
....
....
....
....
....
....
....
....
....
....
....

(but with You by my side, I am comforted!)

I'M FEELING. . .

....
....
....
....
....
....
....
....
....
....
....
....
....
....
....

I NEED YOUR HELP TO. . .

....

....

....

....

....

....

....

....

....

....

....

....

....

Even when life is
difficult, You provide many
blessings, including. . .

....

....

....

....

....

....

Thank You, Father,
for hearing my prayers.
AMEN.

"My grace is sufficient for you, for power
is perfected in weakness." Most gladly, therefore,
I will rather boast about my weaknesses, so the
power of Christ may dwell in me. Therefore I am
well content with weaknesses. . .for Christ's sake;
for when I am weak, then I am strong.

2 CORINTHIANS 12:9–10 NASB

Date:

DEAR HEAVENLY FATHER,

*Today my heart is
troubled because. . .*

*(but with You by my side,
I am comforted!)*

I'M FEELING. . .

I NEED YOUR HELP TO...

....
....
....
....
....
....
....
....
....
....
....
....
....
....
....

Even when life is difficult, You provide many blessings, including...

....
....
....
....
....
....
....
....

Thank You, Father, for hearing my prayers.
AMEN.

"Give, and you will receive. You will be given much. Pressed down, shaken together, and running over, it will spill into your lap. The way you give to others is the way God will give to you."

LUKE 6:38 NCV

Date:

DEAR HEAVENLY FATHER,

Today my heart is troubled because...

(but with You by my side, I am comforted!)

I'M FEELING...

I NEED YOUR HELP TO...

....
....
....
....
....
....
....
....
....
....
....
....

Even when life is difficult, You provide many blessings, including...

....
....
....
....
....
....

Thank You, Father, for hearing my prayers.
AMEN.

It is better to take refuge in the Lord than to trust in man.
PSALM 118:8 NASB

Date:

DEAR HEAVENLY FATHER,

....
....
....
....

Today my heart is troubled because. . .

....
....
....
....
....
....
....
....
....
....
....
....

(but with You by my side, I am comforted!)

I'M FEELING. . .

....
....
....
....
....
....
....
....
....
....
....
....
....
....

I NEED YOUR HELP TO...

....
....
....
....
....
....
....
....
....
....
....
....
....
....
....

Even when life is difficult, You provide many blessings, including...

....
....
....
....
....
....
....
....
....

Thank You, Father, for hearing my prayers.
AMEN.

"Look at the birds of the air: they neither sow nor reap nor gather into barns, and yet your heavenly Father feeds them. Are you not of more value than they?"
MATTHEW 6:26 ESV

Date:

DEAR HEAVENLY FATHER,

Today my heart is troubled because. . .

(but with You by my side, I am comforted!)

I'M FEELING. . .

I NEED YOUR HELP TO...

....
....
....
....
....
....
....
....
....
....
....
....
....
....
....

Even when life is difficult, You provide many blessings, including...

....
....
....
....
....
....
....
....

Thank You, Father, for hearing my prayers.
AMEN.

"I have told you these things, so that
in me you may have peace. In this world
you will have trouble. But take heart!
I have overcome the world."
JOHN 16:33 NIV

Date:

DEAR HEAVENLY FATHER,

....
....
....
....

Today my heart is troubled because. . .

....
....
....
....
....
....
....
....
....
....
....
....

*(but with You by my side,
I am comforted!)*

I'M FEELING. . .

....
....
....
....
....
....
....
....
....
....
....
....
....

I NEED YOUR HELP TO. . .

....
....
....
....
....
....
....
....
....
....
....
....
....
....
....
....
....
....

Even when life is difficult, You provide many blessings, including. . .

....
....
....
....
....
....
....
....

Thank You, Father, for hearing my prayers.
AMEN.

May the God of hope fill you with all joy and peace in believing, so that by the power of the Holy Spirit you may abound in hope.
ROMANS 15:13 ESV

Date:

DEAR HEAVENLY FATHER,

....
....
....
....

Today my heart is troubled because. . .

....
....
....
....
....
....
....
....
....
....
....
....
....

(but with You by my side, I am comforted!)

I'M FEELING. . .

....
....
....
....
....
....
....
....
....
....
....
....
....
....
....
....

I NEED YOUR HELP TO. . .

....
....
....
....
....
....
....
....
....
....
....
....
....
....
....
....
....

Even when life is difficult, You provide many blessings, including. . .

....
....
....
....
....
....
....
....
....

Thank You, Father, for hearing my prayers.
AMEN.

For I am convinced that neither death nor life, neither angels nor demons, neither the present nor the future, nor any powers, neither height nor depth, nor anything else in all creation, will be able to separate us from the love of God that is in Christ Jesus our Lord.

ROMANS 8:38–39 NIV

Date:

DEAR HEAVENLY FATHER,

Today my heart is troubled because. . .

(but with You by my side, I am comforted!)

I'M FEELING. . .

I NEED YOUR HELP TO...

....
....
....
....
....
....
....
....
....
....
....
....
....
....
....

Even when life is difficult, You provide many blessings, including...

....
....
....
....
....
....
....

Thank You, Father, for hearing my prayers.
AMEN.

"For truly, I say to you, if you have faith like a grain of mustard seed, you will say to this mountain, 'Move from here to there,' and it will move, and nothing will be impossible for you."
MATTHEW 17:20 ESV

Date:

DEAR HEAVENLY FATHER,

Today my heart is troubled because. . .

I'M FEELING. . .

(but with You by my side, I am comforted!)

I NEED YOUR HELP TO...

....

....

....

....

....

....

....

....

....

....

....

....

....

....

....

....

....

....

....

Even when life is difficult, You provide many blessings, including...

....

....

....

....

....

....

....

....

....

Thank You, Father, for hearing my prayers.
AMEN.

Trust the LORD with all your heart, and don't depend on your own understanding. Remember the LORD in all you do, and he will give you success.
PROVERBS 3:5–6 NCV

Date:

DEAR HEAVENLY FATHER,

Today my heart is troubled because. . .

(but with You by my side, I am comforted!)

I'M FEELING. . .

I NEED YOUR HELP TO...

....

....

....

....

....

....

....

....

....

....

....

....

....

Even when life is difficult, You provide many blessings, including...

....

....

....

....

....

....

....

Thank You, Father, for hearing my prayers.
AMEN.

"Call to me and I will answer you, and will tell you great and hidden things that you have not known."
JEREMIAH 33:3 ESV

 Date:

DEAR HEAVENLY FATHER,

Today my heart is troubled because. . .

(but with You by my side, I am comforted!)

I'M FEELING. . .

I NEED YOUR HELP TO...

....
....
....
....
....
....
....
....
....
....
....
....
....
....
....

Even when life is difficult, You provide many blessings, including...

....
....
....
....
....
....
....
....
....

Thank You, Father, for hearing my prayers.
AMEN.

For God has not given us a spirit of timidity, but of power and love and discipline.
2 TIMOTHY 1:7 NASB

Date:

DEAR HEAVENLY FATHER,

....
....
....
....

Today my heart is troubled because. . .

....
....
....
....
....
....
....
....
....
....
....
....
....

(but with You by my side, I am comforted!)

I'M FEELING. . .

....
....
....
....
....
....
....
....
....
....
....
....
....
....
....

I NEED YOUR HELP TO...

....
....
....
....
....
....
....
....
....
....
....
....
....
....

Even when life is difficult, You provide many blessings, including...

....
....
....
....
....
....
....
....

Thank You, Father, for hearing my prayers.
AMEN.

Dear friends, do not be surprised at the fiery ordeal that has come on you to test you, as though something strange were happening to you. But rejoice inasmuch as you participate in the sufferings of Christ, so that you may be overjoyed when his glory is revealed.

1 PETER 4:12–13 NIV

Date:

DEAR HEAVENLY FATHER,

Today my heart is troubled because. . .

I'M FEELING. . .

(but with You by my side, I am comforted!)

I NEED YOUR HELP TO...

....

....

....

....

....

....

....

....

....

....

....

....

....

Even when life is difficult, You provide many blessings, including...

....

....

....

....

....

....

....

....

Thank You, Father, for hearing my prayers.
AMEN.

"Come to me, all you who are weary and burdened, and I will give you rest. Take my yoke upon you and learn from me, for I am gentle and humble in heart, and you will find rest for your souls. For my yoke is easy and my burden is light."

MATTHEW 11:28–30 NIV

 Date:

DEAR HEAVENLY FATHER,

Today my heart is troubled because. . .

(but with You by my side, I am comforted!)

I'M FEELING. . .

I NEED YOUR HELP TO. . .

. . . .

. . . .

. . . .

. . . .

. . . .

. . . .

. . . .

. . . .

. . . .

. . . .

. . . .

. . . .

. . . .

Even when life is difficult, You provide many blessings, including. . .

. . . .

. . . .

. . . .

. . . .

. . . .

. . . .

. . . .

Thank You, Father, for hearing my prayers.
AMEN.

The LORD is a refuge for the oppressed, a stronghold in times of trouble.
PSALM 9:9 NIV

 Date:

DEAR HEAVENLY FATHER,

Today my heart is troubled because. . .

(but with You by my side, I am comforted!)

I'M FEELING. . .

I NEED YOUR HELP TO...

....
....
....
....
....
....
....
....
....
....
....
....
....
....
....
....

Even when life is difficult, You provide many blessings, including...

....
....
....
....
....
....
....

Thank You, Father, for hearing my prayers.
AMEN.

"For I am the LORD your God who takes hold of your right hand and says to you, Do not fear; I will help you."
ISAIAH 41:13 NIV

 Date:

DEAR HEAVENLY FATHER,

Today my heart is
troubled because. . .

I'M FEELING. . .

(but with You by my side,
I am comforted!)

I NEED YOUR HELP TO...

....
....
....
....
....
....
....
....
....
....
....
....
....

Even when life is difficult, You provide many blessings, including...

....
....
....
....
....
....

Thank You, Father, for hearing my prayers.
AMEN.

One thing have I asked of the LORD, that I will seek after: that I may dwell in the house of the LORD all the days of my life, to gaze upon the beauty of the LORD and to inquire in his temple.

PSALM 27:4 ESV

Date:

DEAR HEAVENLY FATHER,

Today my heart is troubled because. . .

(but with You by my side, I am comforted!)

I'M FEELING. . .

I NEED YOUR HELP TO...

....
....
....
....
....
....
....
....
....
....
....
....
....

Even when life is difficult, You provide many blessings, including...

....
....
....
....
....
....
....
....

Thank You, Father, for hearing my prayers.
AMEN.

"Blessed are those who are persecuted for righteousness' sake, for theirs is the kingdom of heaven.... Rejoice and be glad, for your reward is great in heaven."

MATTHEW 5:10, 12 ESV

 Date:

DEAR HEAVENLY FATHER,

Today my heart is troubled because. . .

(but with You by my side, I am comforted!)

I'M FEELING. . .

I NEED YOUR HELP TO...

....

....

....

....

....

....

....

....

....

....

....

....

....

....

Even when life is difficult, You provide many blessings, including...

....

....

....

....

....

....

....

Thank You, Father, for hearing my prayers.
AMEN.

No temptation has overtaken you that is not common to man. God is faithful, and he will not let you be tempted beyond your ability, but with the temptation he will also provide the way of escape, that you may be able to endure it.
1 CORINTHIANS 10:13 ESV

 Date:

DEAR HEAVENLY FATHER,

Today my heart is troubled because. . .

I'M FEELING. . .

(but with You by my side, I am comforted!)

I NEED YOUR HELP TO...

....
....
....
....
....
....
....
....
....
....
....
....
....
....
....

Even when life is difficult, You provide many blessings, including...

....
....
....
....
....
....
....
....
....

Thank You, Father, for hearing my prayers.
AMEN.

God has said, "I will never leave you; I will never abandon you."
HEBREWS 13:5 NCV

 Date:

DEAR HEAVENLY FATHER,

....
....
....
....

Today my heart is troubled because. . .

....
....
....
....
....
....
....
....
....
....
....
....

(but with You by my side, I am comforted!)

I'M FEELING. . .

....
....
....
....
....
....
....
....
....
....
....
....
....
....

I NEED YOUR HELP TO. . .

....
....
....
....
....
....
....
....
....
....
....
....
....

Even when life is difficult, You provide many blessings, including. . .

....
....
....
....
....
....
....
....

Thank You, Father, for hearing my prayers.
AMEN.

When I am afraid, I put my trust in you.
Psalm 56:3 NIV

Date:

DEAR HEAVENLY FATHER,

....

....

....

....

*Today my heart is
troubled because. . .*

....

....

....

....

....

....

....

....

....

....

....

*(but with You by my side,
I am comforted!)*

I'M FEELING. . .

....

....

....

....

....

....

....

....

....

....

....

....

....

....

....

I NEED YOUR HELP TO. . .

....
....
....
....
....
....
....
....
....
....
....
....
....

Even when life is difficult, You provide many blessings, including. . .

....
....
....
....
....
....
....
....
....

Thank You, Father, for hearing my prayers.
AMEN.

The Lord makes firm the steps of the one who delights in him; though he may stumble, he will not fall, for the Lord upholds him with his hand.
PSALM 37:23–24 NIV

Date:

DEAR HEAVENLY FATHER,

Today my heart is troubled because. . .

I'M FEELING. . .

(but with You by my side, I am comforted!)

I NEED YOUR HELP TO...

....
....
....
....
....
....
....
....
....
....
....
....
....
....

Even when life is difficult, You provide many blessings, including...

....
....
....
....
....
....
....
....

Thank You, Father, for hearing my prayers.
AMEN.

Yet this I call to mind and therefore I have hope: Because of the LORD's great love we are not consumed, for his compassions never fail. They are new every morning; great is your faithfulness.

LAMENTATIONS 3:21–23 NIV

Date:

DEAR HEAVENLY FATHER,

....

....

....

....

*Today my heart is
troubled because. . .*

....

....

....

....

....

....

....

....

....

....

....

....

*(but with You by my side,
I am comforted!)*

I'M FEELING. . .

....

....

....

....

....

....

....

....

....

....

....

....

....

....

I NEED YOUR HELP TO...

....
....
....
....
....
....
....
....
....
....
....
....
....
....
....
....

Even when life is difficult, You provide many blessings, including...

....
....
....
....
....
....
....
....
....

Thank You, Father, for hearing my prayers.
AMEN.

So faith comes from hearing, and hearing through the word of Christ.
ROMANS 10:17 ESV

Date:

DEAR HEAVENLY FATHER,

Today my heart is troubled because. . .

(but with You by my side, I am comforted!)

I'M FEELING. . .

I NEED YOUR HELP TO...

....

....

....

....

....

....

....

....

....

....

....

....

....

....

....

Even when life is difficult, You provide many blessings, including...

....

....

....

....

....

....

....

Thank You, Father, for hearing my prayers.
AMEN.

Wait for the LORD; be strong, and let your heart take courage; wait for the LORD!
PSALM 27:14 ESV

 Date:

DEAR HEAVENLY FATHER,

....
....
....
....

Today my heart is troubled because. . .

....
....
....
....
....
....
....
....
....
....
....

(but with You by my side, I am comforted!)

I'M FEELING. . .

....
....
....
....
....
....
....
....
....
....
....
....
....
....

I NEED YOUR HELP TO...

....

....

....

....

....

....

....

....

....

....

....

....

....

Even when life is difficult, You provide many blessings, including...

....

....

....

....

....

....

....

Thank You, Father, for hearing my prayers.
AMEN.

"So do not fear, for I am with you;
do not be dismayed, for I am your God.
I will strengthen you and help you; I will
uphold you with my righteous right hand."

ISAIAH 41:10 NIV

 Date:

DEAR HEAVENLY FATHER,

Today my heart is troubled because. . .

(but with You by my side, I am comforted!)

I'M FEELING. . .

I NEED YOUR HELP TO...

....
....
....
....
....
....
....
....
....
....
....
....
....

Even when life is difficult, You provide many blessings, including...

....
....
....
....
....
....
....
....
....

Thank You, Father, for hearing my prayers.
AMEN.

But now, this is what the LORD says—he who created you, Jacob, he who formed you, Israel: "Do not fear, for I have redeemed you; I have summoned you by name; you are mine."
ISAIAH 43:1 NIV

 Date:

DEAR HEAVENLY FATHER,

Today my heart is troubled because. . .

(but with You by my side, I am comforted!)

I'M FEELING. . .

I NEED YOUR HELP TO...

....
....
....
....
....
....
....
....
....
....
....
....
....
....

Even when life is difficult, You provide many blessings, including...

....
....
....
....
....
....
....

Thank You, Father, for hearing my prayers.
AMEN.

"Peace be within your walls and security within your towers!" For my brothers and companions' sake I will say, "Peace be within you!"
PSALM 122:7-8 ESV

Date:

DEAR HEAVENLY FATHER,

....
....
....
....

Today my heart is
troubled because. . .

....
....
....
....
....
....
....
....
....
....
....

*(but with You by my side,
I am comforted!)*

I'M FEELING. . .

....
....
....
....
....
....
....
....
....
....
....
....
....
....

I NEED YOUR HELP TO...

....
....
....
....
....
....
....
....
....
....
....
....
....
....
....

Even when life is difficult, You provide many blessings, including...

....
....
....
....
....
....
....
....

Thank You, Father, for hearing my prayers.
AMEN.

The righteous cry out, and the LORD hears them; he delivers them from all their troubles.
PSALM 34:17 NIV

Date:

DEAR HEAVENLY FATHER,

Today my heart is troubled because. . .

(but with You by my side, I am comforted!)

I'M FEELING. . .

I NEED YOUR HELP TO...

....
....
....
....
....
....
....
....
....
....
....
....
....
....
....
....
....

Even when life is difficult, You provide many blessings, including...

....
....
....
....
....
....

Thank You, Father, for hearing my prayers.
AMEN.

The LORD is good to those whose hope is in him, to the one who seeks him; it is good to wait quietly for the salvation of the LORD.
LAMENTATIONS 3:25–26 NIV

 Date:

DEAR HEAVENLY FATHER,

Today my heart is troubled because. . .

(but with You by my side, I am comforted!)

I'M FEELING. . .

I NEED YOUR HELP TO. . .

....
....
....
....
....
....
....
....
....
....
....
....
....
....
....

Even when life is difficult, You provide many blessings, including. . .

....
....
....
....
....
....
....

Thank You, Father, for hearing my prayers.
AMEN.

But you, LORD, are a shield around me, my glory, the One who lifts my head high.
PSALM 3:3 NIV

Date:

DEAR HEAVENLY FATHER,

Today my heart is troubled because. . .

I'M FEELING. . .

(but with You by my side, I am comforted!)

I NEED YOUR HELP TO...

....
....
....
....
....
....
....
....
....
....
....
....
....
....

Even when life is difficult, You provide many blessings, including...

....
....
....
....
....
....
....

Thank You, Father, for hearing my prayers.
AMEN.

And my God will supply all your needs according to His riches in glory in Christ Jesus.
PHILIPPIANS 4:19 NASB

 Date:

DEAR HEAVENLY FATHER,

Today my heart is troubled because. . .

I'M FEELING. . .

*(but with You by my side,
I am comforted!)*

I NEED YOUR HELP TO...

....

....

....

....

....

....

....

....

....

....

....

....

....

....

....

....

....

Even when life is difficult, You provide many blessings, including...

....

....

....

....

....

....

....

Thank You, Father, for hearing my prayers.
AMEN.

"I will turn their mourning into gladness; I will give them comfort and joy instead of sorrow."
JEREMIAH 31:13 NIV

Date:

DEAR HEAVENLY FATHER,

....
....
....
....

*Today my heart is
troubled because. . .*

....
....
....
....
....
....
....
....
....
....
....
....

*(but with You by my side,
I am comforted!)*

I'M FEELING. . .

....
....
....
....
....
....
....
....
....
....
....
....
....

I NEED YOUR HELP TO...

....
....
....
....
....
....
....
....
....
....
....
....
....
....

Even when life is difficult, You provide many blessings, including...

....
....
....
....
....
....
....
....

Thank You, Father, for hearing my prayers.
AMEN.

For no one is cast off by the Lord forever. Though He brings grief, he will show compassion, so great is his unfailing love.
LAMENTATIONS 3:31–32 NIV

Date:

DEAR HEAVENLY FATHER,

Today my heart is troubled because. . .

(but with You by my side, I am comforted!)

I'M FEELING. . .

I NEED YOUR HELP TO...

....
....
....
....
....
....
....
....
....
....
....
....
....
....
....
....

Even when life is difficult, You provide many blessings, including...

....
....
....
....
....
....
....
....

Thank You, Father, for hearing my prayers.
AMEN.

It is the blessing of the LORD that makes rich, and He adds no sorrow to it.
PROVERBS 10:22 NASB

 Date:

DEAR HEAVENLY FATHER,

Today my heart is troubled because. . .

(but with You by my side, I am comforted!)

I'M FEELING. . .

I NEED YOUR HELP TO...

....
....
....
....
....
....
....
....
....
....
....
....
....
....

Even when life is difficult, You provide many blessings, including...

....
....
....
....
....
....
....

Thank You, Father, for hearing my prayers.
AMEN.

The LORD is my light and my salvation— whom shall I fear? The LORD is the stronghold of my life—of whom shall I be afraid?
PSALM 27:1 NIV

 Date:

DEAR HEAVENLY FATHER,

Today my heart is troubled because. . .

I'M FEELING. . .

*(but with You by my side,
I am comforted!)*

I NEED YOUR HELP TO...

....
....
....
....
....
....
....
....
....
....
....
....
....
....
....
....
....
....
....
....

Even when life is difficult, You provide many blessings, including...

....
....
....
....
....
....
....
....
....
....

Thank You, Father, for hearing my prayers.
AMEN.

Be joyful in hope, patient in affliction, faithful in prayer.
ROMANS 12:12 NIV

Date:

DEAR HEAVENLY FATHER,

....
....
....
....

Today my heart is troubled because. . .

....
....
....
....
....
....
....
....
....
....
....
....

(but with You by my side, I am comforted!)

I'M FEELING. . .

....
....
....
....
....
....
....
....
....
....
....
....
....

I NEED YOUR HELP TO. . .

....
....
....
....
....
....
....
....
....
....
....
....
....
....

Even when life is difficult, You provide many blessings, including. . .

....
....
....
....
....
....
....

Thank You, Father, for hearing my prayers.
AMEN.

He got up, rebuked the wind and said to the waves, "Quiet! Be still!" Then the wind died down and it was completely calm.

MARK 4:39 NIV

Date:

DEAR HEAVENLY FATHER,

*Today my heart is
troubled because. . .*

*(but with You by my side,
I am comforted!)*

I'M FEELING. . .

I NEED YOUR HELP TO. . .

....
....
....
....
....
....
....
....
....
....
....
....
....
....
....
....

Even when life is difficult, You provide many blessings, including. . .

....
....
....
....
....
....

Thank You, Father, for hearing my prayers.
AMEN.

I called on your name, LORD, from the depths of the pit. You heard my plea: "Do not close your ears to my cry for relief."
LAMENTATIONS 3:55–56 NIV

 Date:

DEAR HEAVENLY FATHER,

Today my heart is troubled because. . .

(but with You by my side, I am comforted!)

I'M FEELING. . .

I NEED YOUR HELP TO...

....
....
....
....
....
....
....
....
....
....
....
....
....
....
....
....
....

Even when life is difficult, You provide many blessings, including...

....
....
....
....
....
....
....

Thank You, Father, for hearing my prayers.
AMEN.

And God is able to make all grace abound to you, so that always having all sufficiency in everything, you may have an abundance for every good deed.
2 CORINTHIANS 9:8 NASB

 Date:

DEAR HEAVENLY FATHER,

Today my heart is troubled because. . .

I'M FEELING. . .

(but with You by my side, I am comforted!)

I NEED YOUR HELP TO...

....
....
....
....
....
....
....
....
....
....
....
....
....
....
....
....
....
....

Even when life is difficult, You provide many blessings, including...

....
....
....
....
....
....
....
....
....
....

Thank You, Father, for hearing my prayers.
AMEN.

Praise be to the God and Father of our Lord Jesus Christ, the Father of compassion and the God of all comfort, who comforts us in all our troubles, so that we can comfort those in any trouble with the comfort we ourselves receive from God.

2 CORINTHIANS 1:3–4 NIV

Date:

DEAR HEAVENLY FATHER,

....
....
....
....

*Today my heart is
troubled because. . .*

....
....
....
....
....
....
....
....
....
....
....
....
....

*(but with You by my side,
I am comforted!)*

I'M FEELING. . .

....
....
....
....
....
....
....
....
....
....
....
....
....
....
....
....
....

I NEED YOUR HELP TO. . .

....
....
....
....
....
....
....
....
....
....
....
....
....
....
....
....

Even when life is
difficult, You provide many
blessings, including. . .

....
....
....
....
....
....
....
....

Thank You, Father,
for hearing my prayers.
AMEN.

You came near when I called you,
and you said, "Do not fear."
LAMENTATIONS 3:57 NIV

 *Date:*

DEAR HEAVENLY FATHER,

Today my heart is troubled because. . .

(but with You by my side, I am comforted!)

I'M FEELING. . .

I NEED YOUR HELP TO. . .

....

....

....

....

....

....

....

....

....

....

....

....

....

Even when life is difficult, You provide many blessings, including. . .

....

....

....

....

....

....

....

Thank You, Father, for hearing my prayers.
AMEN.

So that the tested genuineness of your faith—more precious than gold that perishes though it is tested by fire— may be found to result in praise and glory and honor at the revelation of Jesus Christ.
1 PETER 1:7 ESV

 Date:

DEAR HEAVENLY FATHER,

Today my heart is troubled because. . .

(but with You by my side, I am comforted!)

I'M FEELING. . .

I NEED YOUR HELP TO. . .

....

....

....

....

....

....

....

....

....

....

....

....

....

Even when life is difficult, You provide many blessings, including. . .

....

....

....

....

....

....

....

Thank You, Father, for hearing my prayers.
AMEN.

"But blessed is the one who trusts in the LORD, whose confidence is in him. They will be like a tree planted by the water that sends out its roots by the stream. It does not fear when heat comes; its leaves are always green. It has no worries in a year of drought and never fails to bear fruit."

JEREMIAH 17:7–8 NIV

 Date:

DEAR HEAVENLY FATHER,

....
....
....
....

Today my heart is troubled because. . .

....
....
....
....
....
....
....
....
....
....
....
....
....

(but with You by my side, I am comforted!)

I'M FEELING. . .

....
....
....
....
....
....
....
....
....
....
....
....
....

I NEED YOUR HELP TO...

....

....

....

....

....

....

....

....

....

....

....

....

....

Even when life is difficult, You provide many blessings, including...

....

....

....

....

....

....

....

....

Thank You, Father, for hearing my prayers.
AMEN.

We work hard with our own hands. When we are cursed, we bless; when we are persecuted, we endure it.
1 CORINTHIANS 4:12 NIV

Date:

DEAR HEAVENLY FATHER,

....
....
....
....

*Today my heart is
troubled because. . .*

....
....
....
....
....
....
....
....
....
....
....

*(but with You by my side,
I am comforted!)*

I'M FEELING. . .

....
....
....
....
....
....
....
....
....
....
....
....
....
....
....

I NEED YOUR HELP TO. . .

....

....

....

....

....

....

....

....

....

....

....

....

....

....

....

Even when life is difficult, You provide many blessings, including. . .

....

....

....

....

....

....

Thank You, Father, for hearing my prayers.
AMEN.

The LORD is close to the brokenhearted and saves those who are crushed in spirit. The righteous person may have many troubles, but the LORD delivers him from them all.
PSALM 34:18–19 NIV

Date:

DEAR HEAVENLY FATHER,

....

....

....

....

*Today my heart is
troubled because. . .*

....

....

....

....

....

....

....

....

....

....

....

....

*(but with You by my side,
I am comforted!)*

I'M FEELING. . .

....

....

....

....

....

....

....

....

....

....

....

....

....

....

I NEED YOUR HELP TO...

....

....

....

....

....

....

....

....

....

....

....

....

....

Even when life is difficult, You provide many blessings, including...

....

....

....

....

....

....

....

Thank You, Father, for hearing my prayers.
AMEN.

Therefore, my dear brothers and sisters, stand firm. Let nothing move you. Always give yourselves fully to the work of the Lord, because you know that your labor in the Lord is not in vain.
1 CORINTHIANS 15:58 NIV

Date:

DEAR HEAVENLY FATHER,

....

....

....

....

*Today my heart is
troubled because. . .*

....

....

....

....

....

....

....

....

....

....

*(but with You by my side,
I am comforted!)*

I'M FEELING. . .

....

....

....

....

....

....

....

....

....

....

....

....

I NEED YOUR HELP TO. . .

....
....
....
....
....
....
....
....
....
....
....
....
....
....
....
....
....
....

Even when life is difficult, You provide many blessings, including. . .

....
....
....
....
....
....
....
....
....

Thank You, Father,
for hearing my prayers.
AMEN.

*You, Lord, took up my case;
you redeemed my life.*
LAMENTATIONS 3:58 NIV

Date:

DEAR HEAVENLY FATHER,

....
....
....
....

*Today my heart is
troubled because. . .*

....

....

....

....

....

....

....

....

....

....

....

....

....

*(but with You by my side,
I am comforted!)*

I'M FEELING. . .

....

....

....

....

....

....

....

....

....

....

....

....

....

....

....

....

I NEED YOUR HELP TO...

....
....
....
....
....
....
....
....
....
....
....
....
....
....
....
....
....
....
....
....

Even when life is difficult, You provide many blessings, including...

....
....
....
....
....
....
....
....

Thank You, Father, for hearing my prayers.
AMEN.

And he said to them, "Why are you afraid, O you of little faith?" Then he rose and rebuked the winds and the sea, and there was a great calm.
MATTHEW 8:26 ESV

Date:

DEAR HEAVENLY FATHER,

Today my heart is troubled because. . .

(but with You by my side, I am comforted!)

I'M FEELING. . .

I NEED YOUR HELP TO...

....
....
....
....
....
....
....
....
....
....
....
....
....
....
....
....

Even when life is difficult, You provide many blessings, including...

....
....
....
....
....
....
....
....

Thank You, Father, for hearing my prayers.
AMEN.

LORD, you have seen the wrong done to me. Uphold my cause!
LAMENTATIONS 3:59 NIV

Date:

DEAR HEAVENLY FATHER,

....
....
....
....

Today my heart is troubled because. . .

....
....
....
....
....
....
....
....
....
....
....
....
....

(but with You by my side, I am comforted!)

I'M FEELING. . .

....
....
....
....
....
....
....
....
....
....
....
....
....
....

I NEED YOUR HELP TO. . .

....
....
....
....
....
....
....
....
....
....
....
....
....

Even when life is difficult, You provide many blessings, including. . .

....
....
....
....
....
....
....
....

Thank You, Father, for hearing my prayers.
AMEN.

God is not unjust; he will not forget your work and the love you have shown him as you have helped his people and continue to help them.
HEBREWS 6:10 NIV

Date:

DEAR HEAVENLY FATHER,

....
....
....
....

*Today my heart is
troubled because. . .*

....
....
....
....
....
....
....
....
....
....
....

*(but with You by my side,
I am comforted!)*

I'M FEELING. . .

....
....
....
....
....
....
....
....
....
....
....
....
....
....
....
....

I NEED YOUR HELP TO...

....

....

....

....

....

....

....

....

....

....

....

....

....

Even when life is difficult, You provide many blessings, including...

....

....

....

....

....

....

....

Thank You, Father, for hearing my prayers.
AMEN.

Be strong and take heart, all you who hope in the LORD.
PSALM **31:24** NIV

Date:

DEAR HEAVENLY FATHER,

....
....
....
....

*Today my heart is
troubled because. . .*

....

I'M FEELING. . .

....

*(but with You by my side,
I am comforted!)*

I NEED YOUR HELP TO...

....
....
....
....
....
....
....
....
....
....
....
....
....
....
....

Even when life is difficult, You provide many blessings, including...

....
....
....
....
....
....
....

Thank You, Father, for hearing my prayers.
AMEN.

"You keep him in perfect peace
whose mind is stayed on you,
because he trusts in you."
ISAIAH 26:3 ESV

Date:

DEAR HEAVENLY FATHER,

Today my heart is troubled because. . .

(but with You by my side, I am comforted!)

I'M FEELING. . .

I NEED YOUR HELP TO...

....

....

....

....

....

....

....

....

....

....

....

....

....

....

*Even when life is
difficult, You provide many
blessings, including...*

....

....

....

....

....

....

*Thank You, Father,
for hearing my prayers.*
AMEN.

*That is why we labor and strive,
because we have put our hope in the
living God, who is the Savior of all people,
and especially of those who believe.*
1 TIMOTHY 4:10 NIV

Date:

DEAR HEAVENLY FATHER,

*Today my heart is
troubled because. . .*

I'M FEELING. . .

*(but with You by my side,
I am comforted!)*

I NEED YOUR HELP TO...

....
....
....
....
....
....
....
....
....
....
....
....
....

Even when life is difficult, You provide many blessings, including...

....
....
....
....
....
....
....

Thank You, Father, for hearing my prayers.
AMEN.

*My heart is confident in you, O God. . . .
No wonder I can sing your praises! Wake up,
my heart! Wake up, O lyre and harp! I will wake the
dawn with my song. . . . I will sing your praises. . . .
For your unfailing love is as high as the heavens.*
PSALM 57:7–10 NLT

Date:

DEAR HEAVENLY FATHER,

Today my heart is
troubled because. . .

*(but with You by my side,
I am comforted!)*

I'M FEELING. . .

I NEED YOUR HELP TO...

....
....
....
....
....
....
....
....
....
....
....
....
....
....
....
....
....
....

Even when life is difficult, You provide many blessings, including...

....
....
....
....
....
....
....
....
....
....

Thank You, Father, for hearing my prayers.
AMEN.

Delight yourselves in God, yes, find your joy in him at all times. Have a reputation for gentleness, and never forget the nearness of your Lord.
PHILIPPIANS 4:4–5 PHILLIPS

Date:

DEAR HEAVENLY FATHER,

....
....
....
....

Today my heart is troubled because. . .

....
....
....
....
....
....
....
....
....
....
....
....
....

(but with You by my side, I am comforted!)

I'M FEELING. . .

....
....
....
....
....
....
....
....
....
....
....
....
....
....
....

I NEED YOUR HELP TO. . .

....
....
....
....
....
....
....
....
....
....
....
....
....
....
....
....
....
....

Even when life is difficult, You provide many blessings, including. . .

....
....
....
....
....
....
....
....

Thank You, Father, for hearing my prayers.
AMEN.

I have learned to be content, whatever the circumstances may be. I know now how to live when things are difficult and. . .when things are prosperous. In general and in particular I have learned the secret of facing either poverty or plenty.
PHILIPPIANS 4:11–12 PHILLIPS

Date:

DEAR HEAVENLY FATHER,

*Today my heart is
troubled because. . .*

*(but with You by my side,
I am comforted!)*

I'M FEELING. . .

I NEED YOUR HELP TO...

· ·

· ·

· ·

· ·

· ·

· ·

· ·

· ·

· ·

· ·

· ·

Even when life is difficult, You provide many blessings, including...

Thank You, Father, for hearing my prayers.

AMEN.

We can be full of joy here and now even in our trials and troubles. Taken in the right spirit these very things will give us patient endurance; this in turn will develop a mature character, and a character of this sort produces a steady hope, a hope that will never disappoint us.

ROMANS 5:3–4 PHILLIPS

Date:

DEAR HEAVENLY FATHER,

....

....

....

....

Today my heart is troubled because. . .

....

....

....

....

....

....

....

....

....

....

*(but with You by my side,
I am comforted!)*

I'M FEELING. . .

....

....

....

....

....

....

....

....

....

....

....

....

....

I NEED YOUR HELP TO...

....

....

....

....

....

....

....

....

....

....

....

....

....

....

....

Even when life is difficult, You provide many blessings, including...

....

....

....

....

....

....

....

Thank You, Father, for hearing my prayers.
AMEN.

But he's already made it plain how to live, what to do, what GOD is looking for. . . . It's quite simple: Do what is fair and just to your neighbor, be compassionate and loyal in your love, and don't take yourself too seriously—take God seriously.

MICAH 6:8 MSG

Date:

DEAR HEAVENLY FATHER,

Today my heart is troubled because. . .

(but with You by my side, I am comforted!)

I'M FEELING. . .

I NEED YOUR HELP TO...

....
....
....
....
....
....
....
....
....
....
....
....
....
....

Even when life is difficult, You provide many blessings, including...

....
....
....
....
....
....

Thank You, Father, for hearing my prayers.
AMEN.

Now all glory to God, who is able, through his mighty power at work within us, to accomplish infinitely more than we might ask or think.
EPHESIANS 3:20 NLT

 Date:

DEAR HEAVENLY FATHER,

Today my heart is troubled because. . .

(but with You by my side, I am comforted!)

I'M FEELING. . .

I NEED YOUR HELP TO...

....

....

....

....

....

....

....

....

....

....

....

....

....

....

Even when life is difficult, You provide many blessings, including...

....

....

....

....

....

....

....

Thank You, Father, for hearing my prayers.
AMEN.

Date:

DEAR HEAVENLY FATHER,

....

....

....

....

Today my heart is troubled because. . .

....

....

....

....

....

....

....

....

....

....

....

....

(but with You by my side, I am comforted!)

I'M FEELING. . .

....

....

....

....

....

....

....

....

....

....

....

....

....

I NEED YOUR HELP TO...

....
....
....
....
....
....
....
....
....
....
....
....
....
....
....

Even when life is difficult, You provide many blessings, including...

....
....
....
....
....
....
....
....

Thank You, Father, for hearing my prayers.
AMEN.

I know that the LORD is great, that our Lord is greater than all gods.
PSALM 135:5 NIV

Date:

DEAR HEAVENLY FATHER,

....
....
....
....

Today my heart is troubled because. . .

....
....
....
....
....
....
....
....
....
....
....
....

(but with You by my side, I am comforted!)

I'M FEELING. . .

....
....
....
....
....
....
....
....
....
....
....
....
....
....

I NEED YOUR HELP TO. . .

....

....

....

....

....

....

....

....

....

....

....

....

....

....

....

....

*Even when life is
difficult, You provide many
blessings, including. . .*

....

....

....

....

....

....

....

....

*Thank You, Father,
for hearing my prayers.*
AMEN.

*God means what he says. What he says goes.
His powerful Word is sharp as a surgeon's scalpel,
cutting through everything, whether doubt or
defense, laying us open to listen and obey.*
HEBREWS 4:12 MSG

 Date:

DEAR HEAVENLY FATHER,

....
....
....
....

Today my heart is troubled because. . .

....

....

....

....

....

....

....

....

....

....

....

....

(but with You by my side, I am comforted!)

I'M FEELING. . .

....

....

....

....

....

....

....

....

....

....

....

....

....

....

I NEED YOUR HELP TO. . .

....

....

....

....

....

....

....

....

....

....

....

....

....

Even when life is difficult, You provide many blessings, including. . .

....

....

....

....

....

....

....

Thank You, Father, for hearing my prayers.
AMEN.

Behold, I stand at the door and knock; if anyone hears My voice and opens the door, I will come in to him.
REVELATION 3:20 NASB

DISCOVER MORE FAITH MAPS
FOR THE ENTIRE FAMILY. . . .

The Prayer Map for Men
978-1-64352-438-2

The Prayer Map for Women
978-1-68322-557-7

The Prayer Map for Girls
978-1-68322-559-1

The Prayer Map for Boys
978-1-68322-558-4

The Prayer Map for Teens
978-1-68322-556-0

These purposeful prayer journals are a fun and creative way to more fully experience the power of prayer. Each page guides you to write out thoughts, ideas, and lists. . .which then creates a specific "map" for you to follow as you talk to God. Each map includes a spot to record the date, so you can look back on your prayers and see how God has worked in your life. *The Prayer Map* will not only encourage you to spend time talking with God about the things that matter most. . .it will also help you build a healthy spiritual habit of continual prayer for life!

Spiral Bound / $7.99